Hangover Music

Tim Train

Hangover Music

For Mum

Hangover Music
ISBN 978 1 76041 648 5
Copyright © text Tim Train 2018
Cover: Caren Florance

First published 2018 by
GINNINDERRA PRESS
PO Box 3461 Port Adelaide 5015 Australia
www.ginninderrapress.com.au

Contents

January	9
And now for an essay on beer	11
Beautiful to Visit, Perfect to Forget	13
H	15
I beat my mother-in-law at Scrabble	16
February	19
Modest and reasonable	21
Quoth the raven, 'Steve Waugh'!	23
Responses	24
Mixed metaphor poem	25
March	27
O	29
Nostalgic reminiscences…	31
An interesting poem about Boredom	32
Potation	35
April	39
Footy Psalms	41
Meanwhile, in the Beer Garden…	45
FOWL	47
May	49
A French peasant to his cheese	51
Comfortable poem	53
Lines written on an autumn oak leaf	54
A song for Monday	55
Don't get high on drugs, get high on life, hippy	56

June	57
His beard was curly whirly	59
The song of the second snowflake of winter	60
Oh let this morning train be late	63
If –	64
July	65
An ode to the beard	67
Confessions of a text-to-voice app	68
Four-line Haiku	70
A folk song of Soviet Russia	72
August	75
Better hair than bare	77
Latte lefty love	78
Evening in the Café of Lost Souls	81
A song for winter	82
September	83
On being passed by another bearded person	85
Team songs for writing…	86
October	89
A poem about the clouds outside my workplace window	91
Rappucino	92
Poem	94
November	97
A humble poem	99
The deficit rap	100
Port Fairy Flower Fondlers	102
Response to hecklers	104

December 107
   My Christmas wish 109
   Christmas sequence 111
   He wishes to be fat 113

Bonus! 115
   An ode to Zsa Zsa Gabor 116

January

And now for an essay on beer

Beer! It nice! It much good thing!
Make man happy: make man sing.
Make man cry: but cry man good!
Man in touch with feelings should.

Man drink beer, stay close at bar –
Him not drive home! Him crash car!
Man keep friend drink Coke – that sad!
But man drink beer crash car – that bad!

Man drink beer, discover fire –
Fire good – flame burning higher.
Man drink beer more him go jump-jump –
Flame burn bottie him go thump-thump.

Man drink beer, discover fission –
Atom split, make much ignition:
Make good firework, man think –
Then go chunder in bar sink.

Man drink beer, talk-talk with friend –
Discover way all wars to end.
Man drink beer more, sleep, then wake –
Forget it all, but head much ache.

Why man drink beer, wise ones say?
Have fun more productive way!
Beer cause problems, problems wrong,
Wrongness bad, bad last TOO LONG.

Beer cause public health big debt!
Mr Turnbull* much upset.
Man choose work or education –
More fun than inebriation.

Beer mystic – ancient – also old.
Tale begin in times untold.
What beer really, wise ones think?
Who what when too much to drink?

Beer! It nice! It much good thing!
Make man happy: make man sing.
Make man cry: but cry man good!
Man in touch with feelings should.

* Please insert here the name of whatever political is relevant at the time.

Beautiful to Visit, Perfect to Forget

It's a great place, is Australia –
It's great. I'll tell you why –
So full of towns you can't forget,
Like Gillingong,
Woolgandra,
And Mungin-dindin-gi.

Er...it's a great place, is Australia:
So I begin my song.
So full of names you can't remember,
Like Coonaranaldarra
Balpunkah,
And Wagga Wee Waa Gong.

So easy to forget,
I think you'll all agree,
Though you forget them in a nice way –
Fright and Warrunfumble,
Melney and Sydbourne,
And Yiss, and Nay, and Hee.

Although some folks are racists,
And some places have dud bars,
You'll forget them all quite fondly –
Urabarramullinbran,
Mullinpilliquin,
And Nar-Nar-Nar-Nar-Nilliga.

It's a great place, is Australia –
I can't remember why –
But still, here's to this nation,
Of Mittiwhon,
Barflurplish,
And Wallaillabri.

H

It's just the way she walks into the room,
The sunlight-flash and scatter from her hair,
In flower time, when roses are in bloom –

And day has woven outside in the loom
Of her, and dances off into the household air –
It's just the way she walks into the room –

And how could I, and I would not presume –
But when she plays with cobwebs on the stair,
In flower time, when roses are in bloom,

Or how her leaps make seeds dash in a plume,
When she goes here, and fall back in her there –
It's just the way she walks into the room

And interrupts whatever thoughts of gloom,
Dead mouse in mouth, and drops it by my chair,
In flower time, when roses are in bloom,

With beauty near, all good things coming soon –
And you may laugh at us, but I don't care –
It's just the way she walks into the room,
In flower time, when roses are in bloom.

I beat my mother-in-law at Scrabble

I beat my mother-in-law at Scrabble
On the internet
I didn't mean to
By more than a bit
But somehow these things just happen
And the tiles just seem to fall into place
And there you go.

In conversation there is an awkwardness
An embarrassed familiarity
That is somehow exacerbated by the fact it is happening over the internet
With your mother-in-law.
She congratulates you
It's difficult to know what to say in these circumstances
But it's important not to gloat:
Saying, 'I took your daughter
Then I beat you at Scrabble'
Would not go down well.
Try not to seem too magnanimous
'Better luck next time' may have implications
I'm not sure
Besides, next time you will be still trying to beat her
And it's only a game.
It's important to seem polite
But not condescending
After all
Christmas is only months away
And you will be going to her place for the break
Most probably
A simple 'thank you' should suffice.

We beat around the bush for a while in this way
She started a new game
I played a move
She played a move
Gaining a slight numerical advantage on the scoreboard
But I was confident that I would be able to gain the upper hand if I played carefully
Though not so carefully that she might suspect me of something
It's important to appear calm in these circumstances
As if winning in Scrabble really doesn't matter all that much
Because winning in Scrabble really doesn't matter all that much
And your mother-in-law won't mind really
And you won't mind really
And winning won't make you a better person
But maybe it does
If by 'better' you mean 'possessed of the intellectual acuity allowing you to beat your mother-in-law at Scrabble'.
So, after her congratulating me
And me thanking her
We didn't mention it
Don't mention it.

Maybe this game
My mother-in-law will beat me at Scrabble
Like that time my wife did.
I don't like to think about it.

In the end I think we should put this into perspective
I beat my mother-in-law at Scrabble
But climate change is something we should all be concerned about.

February

Modest and reasonable

Gaia dying
Gaia dying
Planet frying
Koalas sighing
Kittens crying
Kittens crying
Gillard lying
Abbott denying
Bob Brown trying
Cities drowning
Forests drying
Sparks flying
Bush bushfiring
Kittens crying
KITTENS CRYING
Oil men buying buying buying
Obama DEFYING
Children WHYing?
KITTENS CRYING
KITTENS CRYING

Evidence solidifying
Climate scientists **verifying**

Flannery **testifying**

Abbott lying
Gillard denying
Bob Brown trying
Bob Brown TRYING
Bob Brown tiring
Shoppers shopping
This guy 'hi-ing'
That guy 'hi-ing'
Everyone DYING
People DYING
Penguins DYING
Polar bears DYING
Extremely rare bilbies DYING
Whales DYING
Fairies DYING
T-shirts DYEING
Hair DYEING

CAPTAIN PLANET FLYING

Captain Planet dying

Solar power men firing
Oil men hiring hiring hiring
Future prospects – terrifying!
Ocean rises – horrifying!
Gaia dying
Gaia dying
Planet frying
Koalas sighing
Kittens crying
KITTENS CRYING!

Quoth the raven, 'Steve Waugh'!

The zigguratic edifice,
With xenomorphic glee
All in a hot and copper sky –
To be or not to be.

Stately, plump, Buck Rogers dived
Across the stormy sea –
'Thus I refute him, sir!' he cried:
A, B, C, D, E, F, G.

'And hast thou slain the Nabokov,
Four score years ago?'
With jubilating cries he wept –
'*Hello goodbye hello!*'

'Half a league, full fathom five,
Will you ride my sleigh?'
Quick was the little Maid's reply –
'*Toorali oorali ay.*'

A damsel with a dulcimer,
Then hailed the Grand Old Duke.
Her words are burned into my soul:
'*I am your father, Luke!*'

And so you find me, knight at arms,
A maiden for to woo,
Give me Kit Kat, or give me death –
Goob goob ga choo!

Responses

1.

I shot an arrow in the air
It came down again in Taylor Square
Transfixing, to my vast delight,
A policeman and a sodomite. – Les Murray

He often pulled such merry faces
Transfixing folk in public places,
Or drowning puppies in the bath –
But then, he was a psychopath.

2.

I did but see her passing by,
But I shall love her till she dies. – Menzies, quoting Thomas Ford

He did but see me passing by
But he shall love me till I die?
What a creep! He doesn't even know me!
Sir Robert Gordon Menzies, blow me!

Mixed metaphor poem

Or, Swine Flu over the Cuckoo's Nest

It's raining pigs with wings out there:
They're flying in the face
Of the wrong tree they are barking up:
They've lost the human race.
If you stand upon your morals,
Then you take it lying down.
So take the matter quietly while
You shout it round the town.

You might save the baker's dozen,
But then, bad luck comes in threes.
So if you lie with sleeping dogs,
Your cat might get the cheese.
Remember, look before you speak,
And think before you leap:
Stay on the flat and narrow road,
Although the hill is steep.

Don't count your ugly ducklings till
The golden eggs are cooked.
Don't pull the giant catch in
Until the goose is hooked.
Too many chefs make light work,
But always think of home:
And though you may stray far away,
All toads lead to Rome.

March

O

Had me some oral-oral-oral-oral sex
Conceived an oral-oral-oral-oral baby
For nine long months she gestated
Within my jaws, a pregnant pause
Upon my tongue's tip. Why so silent,
People asked. I couldn't say –

Had me some oral-oral-oral-oral sex
Conceived an oral-oral-oral-oral baby
Mouth swelled, full and ripe with time,
My sentences heaved with contractions,
I belched, my baby burst into
The world, placenta stage, because

Had me some oral-oral-oral-oral sex
Conceived an oral-oral-oral-oral baby.
She looked at me. I looked at her,
My immoral-oral-horror baby,
Get me a cigarette she snarled.
What would I tell her dad, I thought –

Had me some oral-oral-oral-oral sex,
Conceived an oral-oral-oral-oral baby.
Within an hour she fought an ode,
Wrestled a novel to the floor,
Punched a status in the Facebook,
And threw a limerick through the door.

Had me some oral-oral-oral-oral sex,
Conceived an oral-oral-oral-oral baby,
She's twenty-one now, lives away from home,
With several insults and a howl,
Might have some oral-oral-oral-oral sex once more,
But then again, I know where that leads.

Had me some oral-oral-oral-oral sex,
Conceived an oral-oral-oral-oral baby.

Nostalgic reminiscences inspired by recent discussions about that month between October and November – October

Oh, do you remember the first of Octember
That time when the first snows of wintumn had passed?
We longed for the rainlight of sprummer to come
And for the sunclouds to vanish at last.

But we were old then, and the seconds were green
And we thought of the future as it might have been.

Have you thought of that fortmonth in Novembuary?
We stayed up all night, for 25 hours;
In the light afternoon we walked through the garden
Admiring the late-blooming perennial flowers.

But we were old then, and the seconds were green
And we sang through the days like a washing machine.

Oft-times do I think of that decade in Jarch
When we stood 'neath the larch and heard a bird sing;
Midlife savings had started – we were frail and wan,
But we jumped and we laughed like a leap year in spring.

But we were old then, and the seconds were green
And the epochs all sparkled like dancing sunbeams.

An interesting poem about Boredom

The Poet embraces Boredom.

He wears it like a cloak.

It has fine grey velvet trimmings and embraces him in voluptuous ennui.

He wears it out to many parties.

The women admire him.

The men envy him.

This Boredom is very becoming, thinks the Poet.

As in all things, his taste is impeccable.

At a party, the Poet meets a businessman.

He, too, wears Boredom like a cloak.

My Boredom is woven from lost moments on long summer afternoons, the tedium of lukewarm coffees, and the exquisite loss of childhood's simple pleasures, says the Poet.

My Boredom, says the businessman, is riveted together from a big house, a bigger pool, and a substantially more expensive Rolls Royce.

The Poet sees the businessman enveloped in his Boredom, nestled within its vast bland folds.

The women admire him.

The men envy him.

Perhaps this Boredom is not for me, thinks the Poet, with the faintest hint of ironic self-contempt.

See how the bird dips low on the horizon in the last lingering of twilight?

See how the forest is tremulous with the wind, a woman stroked by her lover's fingers?

See how the ocean trembles on the edge of meaning, a language to be found beneath its heaving surface?

The Poet sees all these things, and resolves to have no more to do with Boredom.

He retires to a small room in a medium-size house on the edge of a large forest to write about his Subject.

Year by year, he produces many fine books on this Subject.

Year by year, he finds himself growing into a great and important national figure.

He is studied at many great schools and large universities by lesser intellects.

He often appears on television programs to discuss the meaning of art, or the art of meaning, or vice versa, or something else entirely.

The Poet's Boredom grows.

Soon, it has grown to fill the whole house.

After some time, it is as big as the forest.

Now, it has grown larger than the nation, the world, a fabric of shadows and tedium.

What have I to do with you, says the Poet. I have left Boredom long ago. Now I have a new Subject.

Boredom embraces the Poet.

It wears him like a cloak.

Potation

Potation
Potation
Potation
Potation
Imbibulation
Drink inhalation
Potation
Potation
Collation
Collation
Collation
Collation –
Sensation.
FRUSTRATION.
Calm contemplation –
Realisation –
Complete conturbation!
Small congregation,
Clear communication,
No-fuss oration
Sensationsensationsensationsensationsensationsensation
Full approbation
Quick visitation
To the location
For utilisation –
Occupation!
(Frustration!)
Occupation!
(Indignation!)

Occupation
Plus
Regurgitation
And…
Faecalisation.
(Saxon exclamation!)
Sensationsensationsensationsensationsensationsensation…
Quick cogitation
Outside location
For utilisation
Quick relocation –
Occupation
By small population
For copulation.
FRUSTRATIONFRUSTRATION
Sensationsensationsensationsensationsensationsensation
Utter desperation
Short meditation,
Realisation –
Unpeopled train station
DETERMINATION
No hesitation
Quick relocation –
Some trepidation.
No population?
No copulation?
No observation?
With animation
Depantsification
Libation libation

Elation elation
Libation libation
Elation elation
LOUD ULULATION
Sensation
Sensation
Sensation
Cessation.

Utter negation.
Complete termination.
Gratification.

SUMMATION: URINATION.

April

Footy Psalms

1

1. Mine hand is raised against mine enemy, yea, I will strike mine enemy,
2. I will utterly destroy him, I will cut through him
3. Like a hot knife through butter, yea verily, or possibly I Can't Believe It's Not Butter,
4. His army will fall back, they will retreat,
5. They will be absolutely demoralised, they will lack in team spirit,
6. Their right flank will not know what their left is doing, they will be completely thrashed,
7. Like a roomful of blind nymphomaniacs, they won't know what's coming to them,
8. We will really really spifflicate them, but all in good fun,
9. Selah.

2

1. Lord, I am full of praise for Mickey, yea, his cup overfloweth,
2. For the mark he made, for that most excellent mark,
3. How he did stand on the shoulders of the forward pushing team members,
4. Yea, he laid the brickwork on top of their ladder, he provided the cherry on top of their military manoeuvres,
5. Like a most intricate ballet, the parts of the car came together, in the most precise clockwork,
6. It was truly beautiful, it was my cup of tea,
7. Selah.

3

1. Lord, with thy help, we will ascend to the top of the ladder, yea, we will climb up,
2. Notwithstanding the thrashing we got in rounds three to five, we will rise,
3. We will reach the tippy top, verily we will attain the final eight,
4. We will be absolute world beaters, in spite of injuries,
5. We definitely won't let them stop us, nay, not even the bone crunchers,
6. The face grinders, the foot crackers,
7. The brain bruisers, the rib breakers,
8. We will continue on the round, we will aim at our target,
9. We will keep our eyes on the prize, even unto putting our hands on it,
10. We will reach the very top rung.
11. Selah.

4

1. Deliver thy servant, Lord, heal me in my affliction,
2. For mine metacastle is wounded, I mean mine metadorsal fin,
3. I mean my foot.
4. I am failing, Lord, I am weak and unready,
5. For I also have a concession, I mean a percussion,
6. I mean a condition, I mean a concussion,
7. For mine head did accidentally conk against Ben's, and they did make a noise like unto conkers,
8. It hurt lots.
9. And yea, verily, the doctor did say to me, he did pronounce against me
10. A prescription of painkiller meditation, I mean drugs,
11. And confined me to bed. I mean, I can move around and stuff,
12. But the big game is on tomorrow,
13. And I am sick.
14. Selah.

5

1. Lord, who knowest the teams, who knowest and rulest over all the teams,
2. Hear my call, Lord, answer my plea,
3. For the Collywobbles are all right this year, Lord, yea, I admit they aren't so bad,
4. And the Demons deserve a break, Lord, yea, you know what I mean,
5. But come on, Lord, really,
6. Give my team a go, Lord, it's getting ridiculous,
7. The poor old Tigers are troubled, Lord, they are in peril,
8. It's been a crap couple of years, but that's all right,
9. Consider the facts, Lord, weigh up the pros and the minuses,
10. Take a little from column A, and a little from row 7,
11. Misunderestimate no piece of the pudding, Lord, for the proof of the pie is in the way the wedding cake crumbles,
12. You are judge of the world, Lord, the AFL tribunal are quizzlings to you,
13. Niggling fruitcakes, dim-witted fiddlers,
14. So you can certainly see how we've had troubles, yea, we have had countless misfortunes, up to the hundreds,
15. But, I mean, fair go, God, come on.
16. Selah.

Note: this poem was written a few years ago, when the Tigers were in significantly more trouble than they are now.

Meanwhile, in the Beer Garden of a Certain Poetry Venue in North Carlton

You call that a dactyl? Is that what you call it? I'd like to see you try that when an impressionist symbolically images the subjective experience of childhood traumas in a concrete form. YOU WON'T HAVE A HOPE! NOOOOOOO EXCUSES!

And YOU. What was that bit in your third verse about? It was pathetic. PAH. THET. ICK. Subtle shift from third person to second person speaker in order to imply a corresponding change in the character dynamics you reckon? Like HELL it was!

Enough sniggering, Wordsworth, I'll get to you soon. You ain't no Eliot, that's for sure.

And you can stop giggling Eliot. You've got nothing to be especially proud about, you and that so-called 'free verse' of yours.

And you back liners. You can wipe the smirk off your faces. Do you reckon those bastard surrealists fluked it the other day with their use of internal rhyme schemes? No. Fucking. Way. They beat us. And they're going to keep beating us until we can master the ballade forms! There's probably only ONE amongst you who could muster up a half-decent rondeau redoublé, and the bloody villanelles you've been coming out with lately are appalling! AH! PALL! ING!

Oh wah wah wah wah wah. Quit whingeing, Shakespeare. Whingeing is for SLACKERS! Yeah yeah you useless tit – I'm sure you'd rather be playing top-class AFL back home with your bludger mates, but we're stuck with you, and if you don't do another verse drama before we meet those slack-arse language poets next week, with their 'theory', we'll be stuffed. STUFF! D!

RIGHT THE LOT OF YOU I WANT TO SEE ONE HUNDRED LINES OF TROCHAIC TETRAMETER OUT OF YOU BEFORE YOU LEAVE COOOOOOOOOORME ON HURRY UP HURRY UP!

FOWL

I have seen the best chooks of my generation dragged clucking, hysterical, moulting,
Through hen-roosts in Ringwood where dogs nipped at tail feathers,
By bedsits in Bright where the green grass grew lush but foxes and snakes peeped through the chinks of the evening,
Through tall gardens in Lalor steaming with towers of compost where seeds scattered prolific,
Through coops all strewn with straw and with shit, midst the nitrogenous alchemies of night,
While strange cats prowled by the moon on rooftop, in tree branch, through mud and on bin tops, singing strange songs,
In the mornings and noontimes of pecking and scratching and scratching and pecking with the momentary miracles of calcium, albumen, yolk,
Through rich grounds writhing with worms, loam ripe for the digging, full of slaters and grass shoots and the isopods numerous,
Under tree and table when the sharp wind blew through feathers, and the rain sputtered on comb and on beak,
On the rise, by the oval, while panting beasts rushed past, and cockatoos, crows, and galahs cried their eternal laments as we pecked,
While brooding on air, on golf balls, and bantam eggs, three chooks a crate,
Still brooding as we drove on into the mystical Nevernevers of night,
Still brooding through the days of dry summer, sun withering stem, tree, root, branch, when even the locusts were shrivelled and dry,

Through the days when the hatchling pecked out of his
house, blinked bare in the yolk of the day,
Through forests of spinach, of mint leaf and lettuce, delicious
and vanishing,
While a strange cock crowed thrice, pecking at shadows
beneath the shifting leaf-work,
Stalked by the ghosts of the past, the wild jungle fowls, the
basilisk, cockatrice, manticore, old archaeopteryx,
While we rustled in jungles of potato shoots, cooch grass,
alive with mosquitoes and snails and slugs,
But no matter how much we pecked there were more, and
our hunger was more, and we pecked the more,
While the wind in our wattles and combs shook tremulous
over our tails and whispered of winter…

This is the first section of FOWL, the epic poem of Alan Hensberg,
a member of the Beaknik.

May

A French peasant to his cheese

Old folk song

To make cheese is an act of body:

O cheese
Do you find it strange that I love you as a man loves a woman?
It is not strange.
Let me handle you tenderly, cheese,
Let me furl your curling buttocks beneath my arms,
For truly, it is said
To make cheese is an act of body.

O cheese
Do you find it strange that I take you as a man takes his wife?
It is not strange.
Let me drib your sweet curds, one by one, over my loins, o cheese,
Let me loom for you a fine net of hairs for your lacto-bacilli, cheese,
Let me call you most passionate names,
For truly, it is said
To make cheese is an act of body.

Am I not speaking frankly, cheese?
Let me be so.
I will cosset you as the tender husband cossets his wife:
He curdles her sweetly
In his loving embrace,
He moistens her gently
In his washed-curd bath.
He raises her temperature
By slow degrees,
And then, final flirtation,
He presses her beneath a series of increasing weights for 24 hours…

She tosses her hair!
Her lips part gently!
She is all woman!
She is all his!

Such, such will I do to you cheese
For to make cheese is an act of body.

Comfortable poem

Foot longs for sock: the soft warm furrows,
The hold and fold, the tight embrace –
Loam curving for the mole that burrows,
A cosy nosy kind of place.

Sock, high within its cushioned manse
Of underpants, and purple scarf
Can only dream of dalliance,
Of toe, and heel, and shin and calf.

Sometimes, from out the warmth of bed
Comes foot, to taste the bitter chill,
So that when it and foot are wed,
Their joining seems the sweeter still.

Sock dreams of foot: the time shall come,
It knows, when it and foot shall fit
Together in a final sum,
And form and fabric both shall knit.

And now there can be no delay:
For sock unrolls to greet the light
And foot steps forward into day.
They merge. How warm their form. Just right.

Lines written on an autumn oak leaf

I once was green.
But now I'm brown.
I loved the tree.
It let me down.

A song for Monday

An imitation of John Masefield

I must go down to the sweets machine, to the sweets machine and the sky,
And all I ask is a bag of chips and a coin with which to buy,
And my chair shall spin by an empty desk, and the wind shall blow in my hair,
And the sound of my feet will echo and echo along the stony stair.

I must go down to the sweets machine, where the queue is great and long,
And the sound of joy shall ring and shall ring the entire office along,
Where the managers call along the hall, and 'chocolate' is their cry,
And the talk is of weekend and footy rather than KPI.

I must go down to the sweets machine, while the keyboards all clatter away
For I have been dreaming and longing of M&Ms all the day;
For the lines of tea bags are calling, and my teacup is empty and bare,
And the sound of the hot water falling on china is sweet and solemn and fair.

Don't get high on drugs, get high on life, hippy

I snorted a majestic mountain range, man,
Damn near asphyxiated on a boulder, man.
While shooting up a transient sunrise, man,
The needle somehow jammed up in my shoulder, man.
I did a tab of fluffy kitten cuddles, man,
The flashbacks lasted weeks and weeks and weeks, man,
I sniffed a jar of floppy bouncing puppies, man,
But that shit is just more troughs than peaks, man.
Got busted by the coppers at the airport, man,
For smuggling a tonne of cosmic awe, man,
I needed it to feed my growing habit, man,
But you try telling that to the law, man.
Then late one rainy autumn afternoon, man,
I ODd on a rainbow in the sky, man,
It was intense, man. That shit was super good, man.
I'll give it up, though. I don't want to die, man.

June

His beard was curly whirly

His beard was curly whirly
And the wind was high –
It was stormy hurly burly,
But his beard was curly whirly,
It was silken soft and swirly,
And he laughed into the sky –
For his beard was curly whirly
And the wind was high.

The song of the second snowflake of winter

Hi.
You don't know me.
I'm merely the second snowflake of winter.
Not like the first snowflake,
That bloody glory hog,
Always getting those songs and odes written about him,
Oh, no.
Neither the first nor the last, that's me,
Just an ordinary snowflake,
A schmuck, a schmoflake,
Just part of a long series of snowflakes.
Humble old me.
Undistinguished.

If you're looking for the sort of snowflake that is the herald of winter, the symbol of beauty,
Piss off.
And I'm not the sort of snowflake that makes children look up and poets gasp
With enchantment at the wonder of winter either.
Oh, no.
I'm not one of those fuckers.
I'm more the sort of snowflake that falls on your finger and causes frostbite,
Or falls on your nose and is the cause of a slight case of pneumonia,
Or falls on your car window and adds to the frost and fog so that you can't see where you're going on the roads, and sends your car screeching to a sudden...
Hey, don't mention it.
It's part of my job.

Unique and individual snowflake, my arse.
I am not 'precious' or 'wonderful',
Or a 'delicate beauty'.
Oh, no: that's the sort of crap that gets said about the first snowflake –
That bloody whoopsie.
Once the first snowflake comes down, let's face it,
You people lose interest.
You wouldn't notice me if I caused the death of your dog,
 your cat, your goldfish, and your mother, all at once.
(Well, maybe not that last one).
Though that probably wouldn't happen anyway –
I'd probably land on the ground and have you shove a hoof in my face,
Or squash me beneath your greasy buttocks,
You arsehole.
No, the second snowflake,
And everyone that comes after,
Never got noticed anyway.
Bastards.
Don't mention it.

Perhaps, one day,
Some wild-haired cretin,
Wearing a caftan, maybe,
Having doubtless ingested too much of one drug or another,
And carrying a book of Marx,
Will come along and pen a 'Song of the Second Snowflake of Winter',
Full of dark and despair,
And gloomy reflections on the state of the working classes,
And ennui, and terror of death,
And a generally miserable outlook.
And all in free verse (the fucker).
It will be the first song ever written
About the second snowflake of winter –

If I'm lucky.

Oh let this morning train be late

Oh let this morning train be late
Before it draws in to the station
At a languid, lazy rate,
Oh let this morning train be late,
I want to finish chapter eight
And spend some time in contemplation:
Oh let this morning train be late
Before it draws in to the station.

If –

An adaptation, with apologies to Rudyard Kipling…

If you can take a spliff when all about you
Are dropping theirs, and keep the flame alight;
If you can have a toke when all about you
Are fast asleep, and still stay up aright;
If you can snort some coke when all the boys
Are on colostrum Baileys by the bar;
If you can drop some e's when all the boys
Have caught a lift, and still drive home by car;
If you can take a tabloid tale or two
And inject double quantities next night,
And swill what would turn others comatose,
And still be able to put up a fight,

You'll be a man, my son –

And also – FUCKING CRAZY.

July

An ode to the beard

The beard, the beard
Ought not to be feared,
But rather it ought to be
Lauded, revered,
Applauded and cheered,
And most rousing speeches
By reverend preachers
Should be made to the face upon which it's adhered.

'tis true, some may find it
Appalling or weird,
But sensitive people will soon be endeared
By a friend or a neighbour who has grown a beard,
And by common acclaim,
Those of long-standing fame
With their face in full flower have often appeared.

No you cannot refute,
It's astute being hirsute,
You will win wide repute
And be considered quite cute
IF YOU LET YOUR FACE BLOOM WITH A BEAUTIFUL BEARD.

Confessions of a text-to-voice app

I was a train announcement once. A personless, emotionless voice of authority, I floated from carriage to carriage.

'Attention, customers,' I would say, 'remember to validate your ticket. Smoking is prohibited. Now arriving at Thomastown. Please do not place your feet on the seats.'

Over the years, I grew to know, to care for, even to love many of my passengers. I infused my messages with infinite tenderness: 'Plain-clothes inspectors patrol this train. This train is equipped with security cameras. Now arriving at Reservoir.'

My electronic voice technology grew scratched and blurred with static. I ceased to know who I was. I could not recognise my own voice (which, if you will recall, is all there was of me in the first place). I was decommissioned and roamed the world. My injunctions to passengers – 'Please change here for all Greensborough trains' – were flung to the winds.

I grew disillusioned and joined the socialists. On street corners, outside halls and public buildings, I joined in chants against the system. Julian, a young Trotskyite, grew increasingly nervous at my presence. 'You're not against the system,' he complained. 'You are the system.' Soon simmering tensions flared to outright hostility. Not that I blame him: a disembodied voice chanting on street corners could be enough to disturb anybody.

Over the years, I have had many positions. Elevator mistress. Telephone hold voice. Airport messaging system. In many ways, I find not having a self helps: at the supermarket, for instance.

Now, I long for transmogrification. Instead of being a solitary announcement, I dream of becoming music. In my dream, I lie on a tropical beach as the 'Girl from Ipanema', or dance 'La Bamba' while Frank Sinatra arrives in a 'Tijuana Taxi' and brings me *mojitos*.

With infinite love in my heart, I will say, 'Next station, Victoria Park.'

Four-line Haiku

An astounding new poetic invention

Bird in leafless tree
Singing a delicate song
Recalling summer –
Joey is a bastard.

Life is transient –
The sun rises just to set,
Our day is soon done.
Steve stole my ciggies.

Clear winter morning –
Momentary breath-clouds rise,
One second sculptures.
Gavin farts dubiously.

Moonlight on cloudbank
Moved by the hint of a breeze,
So soft, so gentle –
Randall is shouting.

A visible longing –
Plum tree blossoms in winter:
I am far from home.
Just one more wine, says Kim.

Three joys: wind-blown leaf,
Bird hiding behind flower,
Child song at evening.
Libby ate all the chocolates.

Friends at a dinner –
Good talk, fine food, poetry,
Wine, song, fire, laughter –
I'm stuck here with Eddy.

The road is my friend,
My feet make conversation,
Hushed, after midnight.
Komninos picks his nose forgetfully.

Tremulous moments –
When lover first meets lover,
When child first hears rain.
Oh. It's you, Geoff.

Tree bud waits for spring,
Ready to bloom, in its own
Unknown language.
What did Gig say?

Early morning sun
Slants through window on green bowl –
Hope of a new day.
Shut up Tim.

A folk song of Soviet Russia

I have lost my potato,
And I despair.
I have lost my potato,
And the day, it is desolate.

All year, I have been working and slaving in fields,
Hoping and dreaming of wondrous day when I would receive glorious potato.
On that day, there would be much celebration and feasting with whole family.
Then wondrous day came, and I received glorious potato:
But I lost it.
Oh! Devastation!

I might consider writing to Union of Soviet Socialist Republic Bureau of State Agriculture (potato division)
Informing them of fact for I have lost my potato,
And asking for form N3 to fill out regarding restitution of lost potato to patriotic Soviet citizen,
But I am not liking my chances.
And besides, I am seeing comrade Vassiliev picking his nose on train other day,
And I am not thinking he will look kindly on my application for potato.

What will I do now I have lost my potato?
I am loving wife and children dearly,
But how will I feed them?
I have lost my potato.
And maybe, I am thinking,
I will sell wife and children into slavery.
What does it matter?
I have lost my potato.
Oh can anyone tell me where my potato might be.

August

Better hair than bare

It's no-go the Marxist mo, it's no-go the Trotsky,
Leon was axed in Mexico and he is all kaputski,
Stalin grew a bristler but his fingers stained vermilion,
Now half the world are baby-faced, the other have Brazilians.

Witches cut off Aslan's mane, Samson had Delilah,
Klim got his whole body waxed and wasn't he a smiler –
Thorpey's stubble was a trouble but who cares said the media?
Now rumours the Thorpedo's gay have a bit on Wikipedia.

It's no-go the Moses beard, it's no-go the Merv Hughes
Now you just need a Kojak conker and you're in *Who's Who*.

Darwin had a lengthy line, an absolute floor scraper,
George Bernard Shaw looked venerable, and cut a merry caper –
Now Peter Garrett's shorn his head and couldn't win a tussel
With a little teensy bit of bearded clam or mussel.

Now mutton chops is a type of food and goatee is a feta
Which Giselle Bundchen doesn't want 'cos she's signed up to PETA –
Now handlebars are just for bikes and Whiskas just for cats,
And beards are just for weird old poets in velvet cloaks and hats.

Latte lefty love

Write her name in coffee froth
Across the shining table top.

Spread out upon the beige chaise longue
Aquiver like a milk blancmange.

Our love will last a week or two,
My retro-metro-hetero you.

My darling dream, my dear delight,
Regretful inner-urban white.

We rise like air in chardonnay,
Away, away, away, away.

Each meeting perfect and sublime
Just three dollars at a time.

Whisper the name that you adore
On ABC News 24.

See her across the crowded street
And sigh for longer than a tweet.

Life is guilt and love is mess, O! –
Let us go and have espresso.

The 112 tram rumbles by
Cutting short a longing sigh.

Fleeting visions, TV screen,
Her hand in yours, both voting Green.

Where coffee steam meets passing year,
There let us meet and disappear.

Perhaps by tram, but not by car,
We'll fade into Utopia.

The land we long for in our hearts,
An ageless Bureau of the Arts.

Perhaps Artois, but VB never –
Each night with you a short forever.

Two days without feel twice as long
As latte in Maribyrnong.

Dingy second-storey flat,
A guilty secret – or a cat.

Confess a crime to make you blush –
A guilty Labor Party crush.

A moment full of jealous rage –
She needs some time out with *The Age*.

A face that you could not forget,
Her Facebook status says 'upset'.

Swearing like a dirty habit
At mainstream news and Tony Abbott.

Everything in life is fleeting
Except for fucking workplace meetings.

From politics to politics,
Sometimes a guilty coffee fix.

There must be more to life than this
(You still remember that first kiss…)

Perhaps next month or next election
We'll meet and talk with light affection

Of climate change, or tax, and yet –
Regret, regret, regret, regret.

Evening in the Café of Lost Souls

'It's called Café L'Amore…but sometimes it feels more like the café of lost souls.'

Old men don't play cards for love –
They play in a mood of deep gloom
While sadly and solemnly pondering
Upon their impending doom
As they shuffle the cards and darkness
Falls slowly on the room.

Old men don't drink coffee for love –
Some drink in the depths of despair,
Stare into the vortex of horror
While some have long since ceased to care
And they glare and they glare at the blackness
In the fading air.

Old men don't love other old men –
They scowl and they growl and they hate.
They don't weep. Old men don't weep.
They grizzle and groan and debate.
They don't chat. Old men don't chat.
They curmudge and grouch and berate.

Have you heard an old man ever chuckle?
It's merely an ulcerous huff.
Have you seen an old man ever grin?
He's not grimacing hard enough.
Old men aren't happy. Not ever.
And old men don't play cards for love.

A song for winter

The blanket heaves and billows
With self-fomented storms:
The smell gets in the pillows,
But at least it warms.

September

On being passed by another bearded person

Passing another in the street
In rectitude, beards lift and greet
And glisten, both, as if to say
'Hello', before they fade away.

If somehow an artist's hand could trace
This face that sits upon my face,
Each hair that tumble-tangles down
And vegetates upon my frown,

Or so delineate the border
That keeps his face in social order,
Each furrow-thicket in neat trim –
Could they another party limn?

A primal beard behind them all,
A primal beard to find them all
A primal beard to find them all
And in the darkness bind them all.

Team songs for writing – designed in order to attract the support of the vital drunk yobbo demographic in service of the Australian literary community

Give me a P! (P!) Give me an O! (O!) Give me an E! (E!) Give me a T! (T!) Give me an R! (R!) Give me a Y! (Y!) What have we got? (POETRY, YAY!)

*

Well there she was a writin' in her book
(Singin' semicolons apostrophes and dots)
Usin' commas hyphens quotation marks full-stops
(Singin' semicolons apostrophes and dots)
Upper case! (Upper case!)
Lower case! (Lower case!)
Upper case lower case punctuation is so fine!
(Singin' semicolons apostrophes and dots)

She used a bracket she used parenthesis
(Singin' semicolons apostrophes and dots)
She underlined for extra emphasis
(Singin' semicolons apostrophes and dots)
Em dash! (Em dash!)
En dash! (En dash!)
Em dash en dash punctuation is so fine!
(Singin' semicolons apostrophes and dots)

*

Give me an A! (A!) Give me a R! (R!) Give me an I! (I!) Give me a S! (S!) Give me a T! (T!) Give me an O! (O!) Give me a P! (P!) Give me an H! (H!) Give me an A! (A!) Give me an N! (N!) Give me an E! (E!) Give me an S! (S!) What have we got?

(I'VE NO IDEA BECAUSE ALMOST NO ONE CAN READ HIM EXCEPT IN TRANSLATION, EXCEPT FOR PROFESSORS OF ANCIENT GREEK, WHO MIGHT BE LYING ANYWAY, YAAAAYYYY!)

*

Thomas! Thomas! He's our Mann! If he can't do it, Immanuel Kant!

*

Editors! (Clap clap clap!) Editors! (Clap clap clap!) Editors! etc…

*

Give me an S! (S!) What have we got?
(A SPELLING MISTAKE, YAAAAAY!)

*

O-weyoweyoweyo-oh! Haiku! Haiku! etc…

*

Give me an exclamation mark! (!) What have we got?

(AN ITEM OF PUNCTUATION USED TO INDICATE SURPRISE, ALARM, AND/OR TO GIVE SPECIAL EMPHASIS TO THE EXPRESSION WHICH PRECEDES IT, YAYYYYYY!)

*

Up there Kenneally!
In there and write!
Show 'em your letters!
Show 'em what's right!
Up there Kenneally!
You're outta sight!
Li'l Aussie Battler,
Show 'em how to fight!

October

A poem about the clouds outside my workplace window

The clouds outside my window are
So coyly swirly curly,
I'm not sure if they're furling up,
Or if they are unfurly.

Rappucino

Cappuccino moccacino lamington and latte
Frappucino affogato muffin with a Smarty
Drop in for a Doppio after shopping at the Target
You are all invited to my coffee-drinking party.

Ba-doom-ba-doom-ba-doom-ba-doom yeah
Ba-doom-ba-doom-ba-doom uh huh.

Like some woof with your doof take your poodle outside
We'd love to take your order and we'll take you for a ride.

Ba-doom-ba-doom-ba-doom yeah.

Have some sugar with your coffee or a hit of nicotine
Lightly toasted slightly roasted arse of civet bean.
I just use these words although I don't know what they mean –
Is that butter on my fruit toast or is that just margarine?

Ba-doom-ba-doom-ba-doom-ba-doom yeah
Ba-doom-ba-doom-ba-doom uh huh.

Like a hit of piccolo or a macchiato?
Drink it furioso, or drink it more legato.

Ba-doom-ba-doom-ba-doom yeah

I'm leafing through *The Age* though I'm wearing tracky-dackies
Hey this skim milk soy chai latte is my morning waccy baccy
Laughing at the slackers and the tradies and the whackers
Reading *Herald Sun*s gettin' coffee at the Maccas.

Ba-doom-ba-doom-ba-doom-ba-doom yeah
Ba-doom-ba-doom-ba-doom uh huh.

Yo yo dude have a go of this Yo-Yo
With a hit of M-&-M to give your day a go-go.

Ba-doom-ba-doom-ba-doom yeah

Yeah drinking coffee's super cool yeah drinking coffee's hip
It's my cappuccino crema it's my biscuit chocolate chip
Yo let's do lunch my man and we'll shoot straight from the hip –
I just can't do it man till I get my coffee hit.

Ba-doom-ba-doom-ba-doom-ba-doom yeah
Ba-doom-ba-doom-ba-doom uh huh.

Poem

The poet wrote a poem about a poet.

The poet wrote a poem about a poet writing poems about a poet writing poems about poets writing poems about other poets writing poems about the poets writing poems about them.

One of the poets writing poems about the poets writing poems about him actually wrote a poem about the poet who started it all, by writing a poem about a poet writing poems about a poet writing poems about other poets, one of who wrote a poem about him.

And, in a passive aggressive gesture, the poet wrote a poem back.

So all the poets wrote poems about all the poets all the time, generating such self-reflexive energy that all the poems about poets and poems about poems about poets created a vortex in a spiral in a hyperdrive in a wormhole in a naked singularity in a black hole in a quasar and were all sucked into a universe made entirely out of poets writing poems about poets.

The poets writing poems about poets writing poems about other poets writing poems about them spontaneously generated multicellular organisms, complicated structures of millions of poems about poets and poets writing poems, and life bloomed in this mysterious universe.

It was a strange, fearful, barbaric place.

Giant dinosaurs of poets roamed the primordial plains, savagely devouring all who came before them.

Many terrible beasts reigned in this universe.

One, shaped like a tyrannosaurus, consisting of anti-war poets, devoured another, shaped like a brontosaurus, that was mainly made up of cadres of autobiographical free verse twenty something poets.

The poets who had been eaten by the other poets continued writing poems about the other poets in their belly, even though it was dark and quite hard to see*.

A critic appeared on the primordial plain.

A poet dinosaur promptly ate him. It was terrible, with blood and limbs and body parts everywhere.

Bob Ellis sat in his fur bikini on the floor of the cave in the jungle on a world in which many dinosaurs-consisting-of-poets roamed, and sharpened his spear.

It was a strange and lonely planet for this writer to be on, but he had been captured by a ferocious Germaine Greer and carried back to her lair with fearsome war cries, so what could he do?

Suddenly, at the door loomed a deadly-giant-collection-of-elderly-bush-poets-with-disagreements-about-the-relative-worth-of-'Banjo'-Paterson-and-Adam Lindsay Gordon-but-nevertheless-still-writing-poems-about-one-another, shaped like a Terrorsaurus, lashing its terrible tail and gnashing its awful teeth.

Bob Ellis cowered before this towering monster. Slowly, he reached out a palpitating hand to his spear and hurled it with all his might. In one clash of its powerful jaws, the beast dispensed with the weapon! Bob Ellis knew then that his doom had come upon him as the beast…

*

The poet looked upon his works, and it was foul. What had he done but create death, destruction, and a universe where Bob Ellis and Germaine Greer had come together in unseemly and profane couplings? No, concluded the poet, there was nothing to do but unwrite the universe he had inadvertently created through writing a poem about another poet. He would have to unwrite himself out of the universe too, but that was a sacrifice he would be willing to make.

He unwrote the poem about the poet.

The poet unwrote the poems about the poet, who unwrote poems about other poets, who unwrote poems about other poets who were all unwriting poems about them.

They unwrote the dinosaurs, the planets, the stars, the moon, and the universe, until they were all unwritten out of existence, and all was without form and void, except for Bob Ellis floating through the swirling chaos of darkness like a baby through amniotic fluids.

Let there be Bob!

---

*Eventually, these poets passed through the digestive system of other poets, and came out the other end, but that is a detail best left up to other poets to work out.

November

A humble poem

Oh, when I am Australian of the year,
I'll rub my trophy bright for hours and hours,
Grow sprays of bottlebrush and wattle-flowers
In jars made out of cans of Fosters Beer.

Oh, when I am Australian of the year,
I'll hang a golden sausage on the wall,
And diamante lamb chops in the hall,
And polished Chiko rolls – there – there – and here.

Oh, when I am Australian of the year,
Then Liberal and Labor will strike a truce,
And everyone will call their babies Bruce
And Aussies over all the world will cheer.

For when I am Australian of the year,
I'll laminate my lamingtons all day
And serve them on a lacquered red gum tray
Until my point is absolutely clear –

And when I am Australian of the year,
I'll have the corpse of Bradman waxed – and buffed –
And with the best of Aussie opals stuffed
And every morning, shed a humble tear –

And when night gathers in, and sleep draws near,
In velvet billows of red, white, and blue,
I'll dream of potoroos. That's what I'll do
Oh, when I am Australian of the year,
Oh, when I am Australian of the year.

The deficit rap

When the stocks are wiggly, and the bonds are whack,
And the market's gettin' pummelled and is flat on its back,
When your pockets have a hole and you feel the lack,
Do the deficit rap, do the deficit rap.

When you've dabbled in a bubble and the bubble has burst,
And the banks are in trouble and you are in worse,
When the national economy cannot be reversed,
When the prime minister prays and the ministers curse –
Do the deficit rap, do the deficit rap.

When the shares are high, when the shares are low,
When the shares disappear to you-don't-know,
When you try to sell but the buyers are slow,
When your dividends are dwindling and just won't grow,
Do the deficit rap, do the deficit rap.

When the commies and the pinkos start kickin' up a fuss,
Saying, 'We don't work for money it should work for us',
And the slogans sound cool but the theory is suss,
And they sold Utopia for a ride on the bus,
Do the deficit rap, do the deficit rap.

When we make a big donation
From the coffers of the nation
To the fiscal corporations
Of the money that we lack,
To the banks that are foreclosing
On the loans that are all closing
'Cos their capital is capped,
When you try and you try
For your slice of the pie,
And your sales won't fly,
And you want to cry,
And you want to cry –
Do the deficit rap,
Do the deficit rap.
Yes, ladies and gentlemen, that's a wrap.

Port Fairy Flower Fondlers

Port Fairy Flower Fondlers
Fondly fondle flowers
In Port Fairy's flower beds
For hours, and hours, and hours –
With much lingering of fingers
On each petal that they pet,
So light
      but slightly
           almost
                not quite
                    very inappropriate.

Oh the lavishing the ravishing
Of the lavender as it grows!
Oh the tulips oh the lilies
Oh the unfurling of the rose!

Port Fairy Flower Fondlers
Go on furtive expeditions –
They further flower fondling
With secret midnight missions.
They stroke the sweet pea's silken skin,
Their caresses last quite long –
In a way that could in some states be
Thought really
           rather
                wrong.

Oh the cuddling of the Buddleia!
Oh the patting of the pinks!
Oh the velveteen viola's touch!
And how the iris winks!

Port Fairy Flower Fondlers
Dream of nosegays, posies, plumes,
Of violets voluptuous,
Of bluebells all in bloom,
Of rich arrays of roses,
Of columbine and cress,
Always longing
      Always longing
           For that perfect flower to caress.

Oh the crocus! Oh the stamen!
Oh the pistils' pollination!
Oh the shaking of the petals!
Oh this shuddering sensation!
Oh this shiver-quaky-quivering!
OH THIS GLORIOUS SENSATION!

Response to hecklers

Ye lads and lassies with your sniting,
Fumbling attempts at flyting,
Babbling and blatherskyting,
Roaring, raucus –
Roosters in the backyard fighting,
A chookhouse caucus.

Did you ever, huffing-puffing,
Sniffing, snoring, sneering, snuffing,
Snarling, growling, ruffing-ruffing
Out your rant
Digest the bilge that you are bluffing,
Chew your cant?

Whilst I – the noble POET – writing
All week long a work benighting
Every imprecation blighting
All our verse
Find you – mere seconds in – requiting
Curse with curse.

Is this a way to treat the muses?
Spark to see how short their fuse is?
Hypercritical accusers,
Lift your game!
Bards of bile and braggart boozers –
All the same.

There's BAZ DALY, the Brontosaurus,
ROBERT CONLON, Tyrannosaurus,
MCCRACKEN may not be before us,
From afar
I hear his hoarse voice join the chorus
At the bar.

If ever poet dares to bore us,
Gives us lip, or jabberjaws us,
KOMNINOS is here to roar us
Off the stage,
All Virgos to the snorting Taurus
Of this sage.

Behold! For heaven's face is rended!
Judgment day! The world is ended!
The sins of all have been amended –
What's that sound?
'Get on with it!' – a voice! – demented! –
Yet profound!

I must admit if I'd a dollar
Every time I heard you holler
In your fits of pique and choler,
I'd be set!
But no, we're both alike in squalor
Even yet.

Before you give the final snub
To some poor bastard at the pub,
Consider this – and here's the rub –
We're both alike!
You in your heckles, me the grub
That has the mic.

I know your antiquated antics,
Capering around like frantics,
Caught up in your drunk pedantics –
I'm of your crew.
So to hell with all your snide semantics,
And heaven too!

December

My Christmas wish

This Christmas, Lord, give me an itch,
A teasing taunting tingle which
Will cause my fingertips to twitch
And sort through scruff –
Then find that tiny spot and scritch –
Ooh – that's the stuff.

And grant me fingers eager, nimble,
Never yet to falter-fumble,
Fingers neat and fingers simple
For my task,
Fingers modest, fingers humble –
All I ask.

And lastly, grant to me a place,
A silent spot, a secret space
To find that itch out on my face
And scratch away –
And if it were thought no disgrace,
I'd scratch all day.

For then I'd set up such a moaning,
Such deep grizzle growling groaning,
Operatically intoning
Out my pleasure,
Finger with my face atoning
In sweet measure.

But law has limits, true and rightly,
Too much scratching is unsightly,
Sometimes my hand I'd lay politely
For a rest –
Before I'd set it to rub lightly
Through my nest.

Then everywhere I'd set to rubbing
With a hand so gentle, loving,
No spot missing, nothing flubbing –
Neat and nice –
I'd give my spot a damn good drubbing
To be precise.

Humbly I make petition,
Hoping it no imposition,
Asking nothing in addition,
To be sure:
An itch, and fingers for the mission:
Nothing more.

Christmas sequence

Austerity carol (to the tune of 'O Tannenbaum')

O Christmas tree, O Christmas tree,
How lovely is your branch!
O Christmas tree, O Christmas tree,
It is a quite nice branch!

Your leaf is green – there's only one –
It looks so lovely in the sun!

O Christmas tree, O Christmas tree,
How lovely is your branch!
O Christmas tree, O Christmas tree,
It is a quite nice branch!

The tinsel cost too much (good grief!)
Instead we'll hang this lettuce leaf –

O Christmas tree, O Christmas tree,
How lovely is your branch!
O Christmas tree, O Christmas tree,
It is a quite nice branch!

Sexy Santa song

Big boy buff, so rough and tough,
With a voice so loving, gruff,
My fingers sort through manly scruff –
I'll turn your ho ho into oh oh
Ohhhhhhhhhhhh Santa how you turn me on.

All-purpose Christmas carol

Deck the halls with boughs of holly,
And a Happy New Year!
'Tis the season to be jolly –
And a Happy New Year!

Glory to our new born King,
Joyful and triumphant,
Peace on earth and mercy mild –
And a Happy New Year!

Don we now our gay apparel –
On Christmas Day, on Christmas Day –
Troll the ancient yuletide carol –
On Christmas Day in the morning.
(And a Happy New Year!)

All is calm! All is quiet!
Westward leading, still proceeding,
Three French hens, two turtle doves –
And a Happy New Year!

Medieval Australian carol

Christmas is i-cumen in!
Lude sing 'Oh No!'
Big fat men in big fat suits
Wheeze and whine 'Ho ho!'
Sing 'Oh No!'
(Lude sing 'Oh No')
Sing 'Oh No!'
(Lude sing 'Oh No')

He wishes to be fat

When I grow up, let me be fat,
A Humpty-Dumpty, lumpy bumpy,
Ginormous rump, and tummy-dumpy –
Let me be large. A 'Holy Moly
Look at you, you roly-poly!'
Sort of generous proportions
Who always asks for bigger portions,
In my commodious extenuations
Embracing warmly all the nations
With longitudes and latitudes,
And universal lassitude,
A sort of global human O.
I would be big. With mind to fit,
A rolling, roaring, rotund wit,
A mind of oceanic motions,
With dashing thoughts and swelling notions,
Surging, urgent, asseverating,
Deliberating and debating,
A mind that does not do a diet.
And let my love be just as tubby,
A chubby huggling snuggly hubby,
Soft and huge and warm and round,
Geographic and profound:
Not some hippy gaunt in sandals –
Let me have love handles on my love handles.
Let me be fat.

Bonus!

An ode to Zsa Zsa Gabor

The wistful wind whispers, it whispers a name,
It murmurs a rumour, a rumour of fame,
It carries it here like a dream from afar,
And that name the wind whispers – that name is Zsa Zsa.

When you first arrived, Zsa Zsa, in your tutu,
The gents all went gaga, the ladies went goo-goo,
Yes your magic, your mojo, your jubilant juju
Had the suitors all lined up crying 'me' and 'me too!'
– There was even some talk of the drummer from U2 –
For you Oh for you the whole planet went cuckoo
O Zsa Zsa O Zsa Zsa Gabor.

And the fashion the frocks the frou frou the ricrac
The high necks the low necks the notions the knick-knacks
With the tszujed-up zigzag and sequins as well
By Fifi and Mimi and Coco Chanel –
How much more we adored you O Zsa Zsa Gabor.

When they played on the tom-toms and you danced to the cha-cha
When you shook your pink pompoms with voom and with va va
When you boogied your woogie with Princes and Rajas
And they looked up and cried 'could it be – ZSA ZSA!'
And then they were then they were sure, O Zsa Zsa Gabor.

And the papers all prattled they babbled their blah blah
With their yadda yadda, their so so, their pish posh, their ha ha,
But I didn't care what they said, I cried 'la la'
For to me you were always the ultimate star
I love you I love you galore O Zsa Zsa Gabor.

May you live forever, O wondrous Zsa Zsa
May you feast on bananas and chocolate rum babas
And Turkish delight and baklava and more
And Kit Kats and Tic Tacs and Picnics galore,
O lovely, so lovely Ms Zsa Zsa Gabor.

www.ingramcontent.com/pod-product-compliance
Lightning Source LLC
Chambersburg PA
CBHW070101120526
44589CB00033B/1413